WELCOME TO
DOOMSDAY

PREFACE BY BILL McKIBBEN

as published in The New York *Review of Books*

NEW YORK REVIEW BOOKS, NEW YORK

THIS IS A NEW YORK REVIEW BOOK

PUBLISHED BY THE NEW YORK REVIEW OF BOOKS

WELCOME TO DOOMSDAY

by Bill Moyers

This edition published in 2006 in the United States of America by
The New York Review of Books, 1755 Broadway, New York, NY 10019
www.nybooks.com

Book and cover design by Milton Glaser, Inc.

Library of Congress Cataloging-in-Publication Data
Moyers, Bill D.
   Welcome to doomsday / by Bill Moyers ; preface by Bill McKibben.
      p. cm. — (New York Review Books collections)
   ISBN 1-59017-209-4 (alk. paper)
   1. Human ecology—Religious aspects—Christianity. 2. Stewardship,
Christian. I. Title. II. Series.
   BT695.5. M69 2006
   304.2'80973090511—dc22

                                                          2006012052

ISBN-10: 1-59017-209-4
ISBN-13: 978-1-59017-209-4

Printed in the United States of America on acid-free paper.

3 5 7 9 10 8 6 4 2

For Henry, Thomas, Nancy, Jassi, and SaraJane
. . . and the future we hope to leave you

CONTENTS

PREFACE

SINCE WE'RE NOW in year six of the Bush administration, it's sometimes possible to forget just how radical the group of men and women running our country really is. They've changed the setting for our political life so comprehensively that indignation slowly gives way to a kind of numbed head-shaking. In the first year of Bush's presidency, for instance, many expressed surprise that lobbyists were literally writing legislation—that senators were inserting blocks of corporate boilerplate directly into American law. Now it just seems like what you'd expect to happen.

Consider last December's climate talks in Montreal. The rest of the developed world came to the conclave determined to figure out what to do when the Kyoto Treaty expired—how to take larger steps toward controlling carbon emissions in the years ahead. It was a rational enough quest—the last decade has seen a steady outpouring of scientific data proving that in global warming the world faces the single greatest threat in human history. With Hurricane Katrina having struck only a few months earlier, one might have expected we'd be ready to talk.

But we weren't. The US delegation opposed any new international agreements. It opposed even holding more conferences to talk about new international agreements. It threatened to walk out of the meeting when Bill Clinton—a former US president, and not exactly a radical on the subject of the environment—was allowed to give an address. The delegation's leader, a man named Harlan Watson who got his job, according to a series of recently uncovered faxes, at the forceful urging of ExxonMobil, made no attempt to hide any of this: "The United States is opposed to any such discussions," he said forthrightly. For that matter, ExxonMobil made no apologies for placing him in his position: "As the largest energy company in the US, [we are] frequently asked by government officials to comment on substantive issues," a spokesman explained. "We take that responsibility seriously." Did this revelation startle anyone else? No, of course it didn't. Six years into the Bush administration, we all but take it for granted that this is how it works.

But how did it happen? The natural give-and-take between industry and scientists has marked environmental policy for decades: the research always suggests we need cleaner air or water, the executives always suggest it will be too expensive, and somewhere in the middle a consensus emerges. That's what happens in Germany and Britain and even Sweden—in any democracy. But the Bush years have been marked by a complete lack of interest in such consensus.

And what Bill Moyers demonstrates in this essay is one reason why: there's a zeal on the right that comes, in some measure at least, from the sense that we live in special times. Not special times because over the course of decades we've been raising the temperature of the planet higher than it's been for tens of millions of years. Special times because—and 44 percent of Americans would agree with this, according to one recent poll—Jesus will come within our lifetimes to lift his followers up to heaven. And that zeal reaches into the very center of our political life.

Take the case of Senator James Inhofe (R-Okla.). It's no secret he's a fervent evangelical. He claimed on the Senate floor, for instance, that the West Bank and Gaza are "rightfully Israel's land," using Scripture as proof, and he referred to the 1993 Oslo accord as a "tragic occasion."

Inhofe is a minor player in international affairs. But in environmental matters, it's a different story. As chair of the Senate Committee on Energy and Natural Resources, he controls the fate of any legislation that might make even the smallest attempt to control carbon emissions. That fate is never in doubt—Inhofe has called the idea that human beings might be warming the planet "the greatest hoax ever perpetrated on the American people." Last fall, when his committee ran short of industry "scientists" willing to debunk the overwhelming scientific consensus about climate change, Inhofe instead turned to novelist Michael Crichton, whose thriller *State of Fear* postulated that the entire matter was an invention of environmentalists looking for donations.

A few weeks later, when Richard Cizik, a leader of the National Evangelical Association, said his group was considering joining in the fight against global warming on the grounds of defending God's creation, Inhofe told *The New York Times* that they had been "'led down a liberal path' by environmentalists and others who have convinced the group that issues like poverty and the environment are worth their efforts." "You can always find in Scriptures a passage to misquote for almost anything," Inhofe said in an interview, dismissing the position of Mr. Cizik's association as "something very strange."

More than any other public figure Bill Moyers has waded into this battle, and given far better than he's got. Now that Bush's popularity has begun to fade and reporters have begun, timidly, to resume something of their traditional role, it's easy to forget just how cowed everyone was in the years after September 11. Only a few people dared to even suggest that the emperor was clad in a Speedo—Paul Krugman in *The New York Times*, say. On television, Moyers was the sole such voice. His PBS program *NOW* was not wildly political, but by performing the traditional journalistic job of looking skeptically at the powerful, and looking realistically at the results of government policies on people and nature, he managed to run spectacularly afoul of the powers that be. We now know that the Republican appointee to run the Corporation for Public Broadcasting, Kenneth Tomlinson, was obsessed with Moyers's show, to the point of hiring a semiliterate detective to analyze whether its guests tilted "pro-Bush" or not.

With Moyers's retirement from TV journalism, he has felt increasingly free to state precisely what he thinks—to, in effect, start declaring the conclusions he's reached in a career spent in behind-the-scenes politics and in journalism. His speeches have become extremely popular, drawing sellout crowds across the nation, even (maybe especially) in red-state cities where his listeners feel especially lonely.

They are among the most-reproduced items on the Web (well, among the most-reproduced fully clothed items on the Web). And one reason, surely, is that he pulls no punches. In the talk published here, for instance, he calls the idea of the Rapture "bizarre," which it surely is. But how does he dare do that? How can a right-thinking American ever disparage someone else's religious beliefs?

An integral part of his confidence, I would submit, comes from his background. Moyers was trained at a Texas Baptist seminary. Indeed he was ordained to preach. The Bible is therefore not the obscure document to him that it is to many liberals. He knows that the story of the Rapture, far from being central to Scripture, is instead "a fantastical theology concocted in the nineteenth century by two immigrant preachers who took disparate passages from the Bible and wove them with their own hallucinations into a narrative foretelling the return of Jesus and the end of the world." Equally to the point, he knows that the gospels are in fact radical in a very different way—that they command a just distribution of the world's goods, that they demand the poor be succored, that they foresee not an individual-istic rapture of the smug but what Martin Luther King Jr. called a "beloved community" here on earth.

Moyers, it seems to me, knows a powerful truth—that progressives should have surrendered neither the Bible nor the flag to their opponents. His understanding of America's history is at least as deep as his understanding of Christian tradition. In particular, his speeches return time and again to the promise implicit in America's founding that we are a nation of equals, not a snakepit where the wealthy use their money to win tax cuts and to snatch away the hard-earned gains (like Social Security, for instance) of the rest of us. With his feet firmly planted in the deepest American traditions, he can swing back at the right with full force.

The final, and most telling, irony is that he turns not only the sources of the zealous right against them but also the forms. For Moyers in this last phase of his career is preaching, and preaching with exemplary power. Helping keep alive, in fact, an oratorical tradition that is fading after two centuries. Trained by his career in broadcasting, he writes for the ear, his cadences and his repetitions timed to bring an audience to full realization of its role and its power. Focus on the last third of the talk that follows, with its sequence of paragraphs that start "I read," with its peroration about "the will to fight" as "the antidote for despair, the cure for cynicism, and the answer to those faces looking back at me from the photographs on my desk." Forget Pat Robertson and Jerry Falwell—Bill Moyers is giving some of the most wrenching and most important sermons of our age.

—BILL MCKIBBEN

WELCOME TO
DOOMSDAY

As published in *The New York Review of Books*
March 24, 2005

WELCOME TO DOOMSDAY

THERE ARE TIMES when what we journalists see and intend to write about dispassionately sends a shiver down the spine, shaking us from our neutrality. This has been happening to me frequently of late as one story after another drives home the fact that the delusional is no longer marginal but has come in from the fringe to influence the seats of power. We are witnessing today a coupling of ideology and theology that threatens our ability to meet the growing ecological crisis. Theology asserts propositions that need not be proven true, while ideologues hold stoutly to a worldview despite being contradicted by what is generally accepted as reality. The combination can make it impossible for a democracy to fashion real-world solutions to otherwise intractable challenges.

In the just-concluded election cycle, as Mark Silk writes in *Religion in the News*,

1.

the assiduous cultivation of religious constituencies by the Bush apparat, and the undisguised intrusion of evangelical leaders and some conservative Catholic hierarchs into the presidential campaign, demonstrated that the old rule of maintaining a decent respect for the nonpartisanship of religion can now be broken with impunity.

The result is what the Italian scholar Emilio Gentile, quoted in Silk's newsletter, calls "political religion"—"religion as an instrument of domestic political combat." On gay marriage and abortion—the most conspicuous of the "nonnegotiable" items in a widely distributed Catholic voter's guide—no one should be surprised what this political religion portends. The agenda has been foreshadowed for years, ever since Jerry Falwell, Pat Robertson, and other right-wing Protestants set out to turn white evangelicals into a solid Republican voting bloc and reached out to make allies of their former antagonists, conservative Catholics.

What has been less apparent is the impact of the new political religion on environmental policy. Evangelical Christians have been divided. Some were indifferent. The majority of conservative evangelicals, on the other hand, have long hooked their view to the account in the first book of the Bible:

> So God created man in his own image, in the image of God he created him; male and female he created them. And God blessed them, and God said to them, "Be fruitful and multiply, and fill the earth and subdue it; and have dominion over the fish of the sea and over the birds of the air and over every living thing that moves upon the earth."

There are widely varying interpretations of this text, but it is safe to say that all presume human beings have inherited the earth to be used as they see fit. For many, God's gift to Adam and Eve of "dominion" over the earth and all its creatures has been taken as the right to unlimited exploitation. But as Blaine Harden reported recently in *The Washington Post*, some evangelicals are beginning to "go for the green." Last October the National Association of Evangelicals adopted an "Evangelical Call to Civic Responsibility," affirming that "God-given dominion is a sacred responsibility to steward the earth and not a license to abuse the creation of which we are a part." The declaration acknowledged that for the sake of clean air, clean water, and adequate resources, the government "has an obligation to protect its citizens from the effects of environmental degradation."

But even for green activists in evangelical circles, Harden wrote, "there are landmines."

Welcome to the Rapture!

There are millions of Christians who believe the Bible is literally true, word for word. Some of them—we'll come back to the question of how many—subscribe to a fantastical theology concocted in the nineteenth century by two immigrant preachers who took disparate passages from the Bible and wove them with their own hallucinations into a narrative foretelling the return of Jesus and the end of the world. Google the "Rapture Index" and you will see just how the notion has seized the imagination of many a good and sincere believer (you will also see just where we stand right now in the ticking of the clock toward the culmination of history in the Apocalypse). It is the inspiration for the best-selling books in America today—the twelve novels in the Left Behind series by Christian fundamentalist and religious-right warrior Tim LaHaye, a co-founder with Jerry Falwell of the Moral Majority.

The plot of the Rapture—the word never appears in the Bible although some fantasists insist it is the hidden code to the Book of Revelation—is rather simple, if bizarre. (The British writer George Monbiot recently did a brilliant dissection of it and I am indebted to him for refreshing my own insights.) Once Israel has occupied the rest of its "biblical lands," legions of the Antichrist will attack it, triggering a final showdown in the valley of Armageddon. As the Jews who have not been converted are burned the Messiah will return for the Rapture. True believers will be transported to heaven where, seated at the right hand of God, they will watch their political and religious opponents writhe in the misery of plagues—boils, sores, locusts, and frogs—during the several years of tribulation that follow.

I'm not making this up. Like Monbiot, I read the literature, including *The Rapture Exposed*, a recent book by Barbara Rossing, who teaches the New Testament at the Lutheran School of Theology at Chicago, and *America Right or Wrong*, by Anatol Lieven, senior associate at the Carnegie Endowment for International Peace. On my weekly broadcast for PBS, we reported on these true believers, following some of them from Texas to the West Bank. They are sincere, serious, and polite as they tell you they feel called to help bring the Rapture on as fulfillment of biblical prophecy. To this end they have declared solidarity with Israel and the Jewish settlements and backed up their support with money and volunteers.

For them the invasion of Iraq was a warm-up act, predicted in the Book of Revelation, where four angels "bound in the great river Euphrates" will be released "to slay the third part of man." A war with Islam in the Middle East is not something to be feared but welcomed—an essential conflagration on the road to redemption. The last time I Googled it, the Rapture Index stood at 144— approaching the critical threshold when the prophesy is fulfilled, the whole thing blows, the Son of God returns, and the righteous enter paradise while sinners will be condemned to eternal hellfire.

What does this mean for public policy and the environment? Listen to John Hagee, pastor of the 17,000-member Cornerstone Church in San Antonio, who is quoted in Rossing's book as saying: "Mark it down, take it to heart, and comfort one another with these words. Doomsday is coming for the earth, for the nations, and for individuals, but those who have trusted in Jesus will not be present on earth to witness the dire time of tribulation." Rossing sums up the message in five words that she says are basic Rapture credo: "The world cannot be saved." It leads to "appalling ethics," she reasons, because the faithful are relieved of concern for the environment, violence, and everything else except their personal salvation. The earth suffers the same fate as the unsaved. All are destroyed.

How many true believers are there? It's impossible to pin down. A recent ABC *Primetime* poll found that six in ten Americans surveyed consider biblical accounts such as those about God's creation of the world in six days and Noah's Ark to be true, "word for word." And there is a constituency for the End Times. A *Newsweek* poll found that 36 percent of respondents held the Book of Revelation to be "true prophecy." (A *Time*/CNN poll reported that one quarter think the Bible predicted the 9/11 attacks.) Drive across the country with your radio tuned to some of the 1,600

Christian radio stations or turn to some of the 250 Christian
TV stations and you can hear the Gospel of the Apocalypse
in sermon and song. Or go, as *The Toronto Star's* Tom Harpur
did, to the Florida Panhandle where he came across an all-
day conference "at one of the largest Protestant churches I
have ever been in," the Village Baptist Church in Destin. The
theme of the day was "Left Behind: A Conference on Biblical
Prophecy about End Times" and among the speakers were
none other than Tim LaHaye and two other leading voices in
the religious right today, Gary Frazier and Ed Hindson. Here
is what Harpur wrote for his newspaper:

> I have never heard so much venom and dangerous
> ignorance spouted before an utterly unquestioning,
> otherwise normal-looking crowd in my life....
> There were stunning statements about humans hav-
> ing been only 6,000 years on Earth and other
> denials of contemporary geology and biology. And
> we learned that the Rapture, which could happen

any second now, but certainly within the next 40
years, will instantly sweep all the "saved" Americans
(perhaps one-half the population) to heaven. . . .

But these fantasies were harmless compared with the
hatred against Islam that followed. Here are some direct
quotes: "Islam is an intolerant religion—and it's clear
whose side we should be on in the Middle East." Applause
greeted these words: "Allah and Jehovah are not the same
God. . . . Islam is a Satanic religion. . . . They're going to
attack Israel for certain. . . ." Gary Frazier shouted at the top
of his lungs: "Wake Up! Wake Up!" And roughly eight
hundred heads (at $25.00 per) nodded approval as he
added that the left-wing, anti-Israel media—"for example,
CNN"—will never tell the world the truth about Islam.
According to these three, and the millions of Americans
they lead, Muslims intend ultimately "to impose their religion on us all." It was clear, Harpur wrote: "A terrible, final
war in the region is inevitable."

You can understand why people in the grip of such fantasies cannot be expected to worry about the environment. As Glenn Scherer writes in his report for the on-line environmental magazine Grist, why care about the earth when the droughts, floods, famine, and pestilence brought by ecological collapse are signs of the apocalypse foretold in the Bible? Why care about global climate change when you and yours will be rescued in the Rapture? Why bother to convert to alternative sources of energy and reduce dependence on oil from the volatile Middle East? Anyway, until Christ does return, the Lord will provide.

Scherer came upon a high school history book, America's Providential History, which is used in fundamentalist circles. Students are told that "the secular or socialist has a limited resource mentality and views the world as a pie that needs to be cut up so everyone can get a piece." The Christian, however, "knows that the potential in God is unlimited and that there is no shortage of resources in God's Earth. . . . While many secularists view the world as overpopulated, Christians know that God has made the earth sufficiently large with plenty of resources to accommodate all of the people."

While it is impossible to know how many people hold these views, we do know that fundamentalists constitute a large and powerful proportion of the Republican base, and, as Anatol Lieven writes, "fundamentalist religiosity has become an integral part of the radicalization of the right in the US and of the tendency to demonize political opponents as traitors and enemies of God and America"—including, one must note, environmentalists, who are routinely castigated as villains and worse by the right. No wonder Karl Rove wandered the White House whistling "Onward Christian Soldiers" as he prepared for the 2004 elections.

 I am not suggesting that fundamentalists are running the government, but they constitute a significant force in the coalition that now holds a monopoly of power in Washington under a Republican Party that for a generation has been moved steadily to the right by its more extreme variants even as it has become more and more beholden to the corporations that finance it. One is foolish to think that their bizarre ideas do not matter. I have no idea what President Bush thinks of the fundamentalists' fantastical theology, but he would not be president without them. He suffuses his language with images and metaphors they appreciate, and they were bound to say amen when Bob Woodward reported that the President "was casting his vision, and that of the country, in the grand vision of God's master plan."

That will mean one thing to Dick Cheney and another to Tim LaHaye, but it will confirm their fraternity in a regime whose chief characteristics are ideological disdain for evidence and theological distrust of science. Many of the constituencies who make up this alliance don't see eye to eye on many things, but for President Bush's master plan for rolling back environmental protections they are united. A powerful current connects the administration's multinational corporate cronies who regard the environment as ripe for the picking and a hard-core constituency of fundamentalists who regard the environment as fuel for the fire that is coming. Once again, populist religion winds up serving the interests of economic elites.

The corporate, political, and religious right's hammer-lock on environmental policy extends to the US Congress. Nearly half of its members before the election—231 legislators in all (more since the election)—are backed by the religious right, which includes several powerful fundamentalist leaders like LaHaye. Forty-five senators and 186 members of the 108th Congress earned 80 to 100 percent approval ratings from the most influential Christian right advocacy groups. Not one includes the environment as one of their celebrated "moral values."

When I talk about this before a live audience I can see from the look on the faces before me just how hard it is for a journalist to report on such things with any credibility. So let me put on a personal level what sends the shiver down my spine.

I myself don't know how to be in this world without expecting a confident future and getting up every morning to do what I can to bring it about. I confess to having always been an optimist. Now, however, I remember my friend on Wall Street whom I once asked, "What do you think of the market?" "I'm optimistic," he answered. "Then why do you look so worried?" And he answered, "Because I am not sure my optimism is justified."

I'm not, either. Once upon a time I believed that people will protect the natural environment when they realize its importance to their health and to the health and lives of their children. Now I am not so sure. It's not that I don't want to believe this—it's just that as a journalist I have been trained to read the news and connect the dots.

I read that the administrator of the US Environmental Protection Agency has declared the election a mandate for President Bush on the environment. This for an administration:

- that wants to rewrite the Clean Air Act, the Clean Water Act, and the Endangered Species Act protecting rare plant and animal species and their habitats, as well as the national Environmental Policy Act that requires the government to judge beforehand if actions might damage natural resources;

- that wants to relax pollution limits for ozone, eliminate vehicle tailpipe inspections, and ease pollution standards for cars, sport utility vehicles, and diesel-powered big trucks and heavy equipment;

- that wants a new international audit law to allow corporations to keep certain information about environmental problems secret from the public;

- that wants to drop all its New-Source Review suits against polluting coal-fired power plans and weaken consent decrees reached earlier with coal companies;

- that wants to open the Arctic National Wildlife Refuge to drilling and increase drilling in Padre Island National Seashore, the longest stretch of undeveloped barrier island in the world and the last great coastal wild land in America;

- that is radically changing the management of our national forests to eliminate critical environmental reviews, open them to new roads, and give the timber companies a green light to slash and cut as they please.

I read the news and learned how the Environmental Protection Agency plotted to spend $9 million—$2 million of it from the President's friends at the American Chemistry Council—to pay poor families to continue the use of pesticides in their homes. These pesticides have been linked to neurological damage in children, but instead of ordering an end to their use, the government and the industry concocted a scheme to offer the families $970 each, as well as a camcorder and children's clothing, to serve as guinea pigs for the study.

I read that President Bush has more than one hundred high-level officials in his administration overseeing industries they once represented as lobbyists, lawyers, or corporate advocates—company insiders waved through the revolving door of government to assure that drug laws, food policies, land use, and the regulation of air pollution are industry-friendly. Among the "advocates-turned-regulators" are a former meat industry lobbyist who helps decide how meat is labeled; a former drug company lobbyist who influences prescription drug policies; a former energy lobbyist who, while accepting payments for bringing clients into his old lobbying firm, helps to determine how much of our public lands those former clients can use for oil and gas drilling.

I read that civil penalties imposed by the Environmental Protection Agency against polluters in 2004 hit a fifteen-year low, in what amounts to an extended holiday for industry from effective compliance with environmental laws.

I read that the administration's allies at the International Policy Network, which is supported by ExxonMobil and others of like mind and interest, have issued a report describing global warming as "a myth" at practically the same time the President, who earlier rejected the international treaty outlining limits on greenhouse gases, wants to prevent any "written or oral report" from being issued by any international meetings on the issue.

I read not only the news but the fine print of a recent appropriations bill passed by Congress, with obscure amendments removing all endangered species protections from pesticides, prohibiting judicial review for a forest in

Oregon, waiving environmental review for grazing permits on public lands, and weakening protection against development for crucial habitats in California.

I read all this and look up at the pictures on my desk, next to the computer—pictures of my grandchildren: Henry, age twelve; Thomas, ten; Nancy, eight; Jassi, three; SaraJane, one. I see the future looking back at me from those photographs and I say, "Father, forgive us, for we know not what we do." And then the shiver runs down my spine and I am seized by the realization: "That's not right. We do know what we are doing. We are stealing their future. Betraying their trust. Despoiling their world."

And I ask myself: Why? Is it because we don't care? Because we are greedy? Because we have lost our capacity for outrage, our ability to sustain indignation at injustice?

What has happened to our moral imagination?

On the heath Lear asks Gloucester: "How do you see the world?" And Gloucester, who is blind, answers: "I see it feelingly."

I see it feelingly.

Why don't we feel the world enough to save it—for our kin to come?

The news is not good these days. But as a journalist I know the news is never the end of the story. The news can be the truth that sets us free not only to feel but to fight for the future we want. The will to fight is the antidote to despair, the cure for cynicism, and the answer to those faces looking back at me from those photographs on my desk. We must match the science of human health to what the ancient Israelites called *hochma*—the science of the heart, the capacity to see and feel and then to act as if the future depended on us.

Believe me, it does.

**Fear and Loathing in
George W. Bush's Washington**
by Elizabeth Drew
Preface by Russell Baker

**Glory and Terror:
The Growing Nuclear Danger**
by Steven Weinberg
Preface by Anthony Lewis

Fixed Ideas: America Since 9.11
by Joan Didion
Preface by Frank Rich

*Available from your local bookseller
or at nyrb.com*

The New York Review of Books